Wild Things

Animals of the Ocean

By Czeena Devera

 A dolphin swims in the ocean.

A turtle swims in the ocean.

 A whale swims in the ocean.

A shark swims in the ocean.

An otter swims in the ocean.

A jellyfish swims in the ocean.

A seal swims in the ocean.

A squid swims in the ocean.

 A manatee swims in the ocean.

A sea horse swims in the ocean.

A walrus swims in the ocean.

An eel swims in the ocean.

Word List

sight words

dolphin	shark	manatee
swims	otter	sea horse
ocean	jellyfish	walrus
turtle	seal	eel
whale	squid	

73 Words

A dolphin swims in the ocean.
A turtle swims in the ocean.
A whale swims in the ocean.
A shark swims in the ocean.
An otter swims in the ocean.
A jellyfish swims in the ocean.
A seal swims in the ocean.
A squid swims in the ocean.
A manatee swims in the ocean.
A sea horse swims in the ocean.
A walrus swims in the ocean.
An eel swims in the ocean.

Published in the United States of America by Cherry Lake Publishing
Ann Arbor, Michigan
www.cherrylakepublishing.com

Photo Credits: ©Rich Carey /Shutterstock.com, front cover; ©By Neirfy /Shutterstock.com, 1; ©Matt9122 / Shutterstock.com, 2; ©Shane Myers Photography /Shutterstock.com, 3; ©Paul S. Wolf /Shutterstock.com, 4; ©VisionDive /Shutterstock.com, 5; ©Joel Shawn /Shutterstock.com, 6; ©Valerio D'Ambrogi /Shutterstock.com, 7; ©Pat Stornebrink /Shutterstock.com, 8; ©George P Gross /Shutterstock.com, 9; ©gary powell /Shutterstock.com, 10; ©Yakov Oskanov /Shutterstock.com, 11; ©jo Crebbin /Shutterstock.com, 12; ©Marty Wakat /Shutterstock.com, 13; ©Eric Isselee /Shutterstock.com, 15, back cover

Cherry Blossom Press is an imprint of Cherry Lake Publishing.

Library of Congress Cataloging-in-Publication Data

Names: Devera, Czeena, author.
Title: Animals of the ocean / by Czeena Devera.
Description: Ann Arbor : Cherry Lake Publishing, [2019] | Series: Wild things | Audience: Pre-school, excluding K.
Identifiers: LCCN 2019006019| ISBN 9781534149809 (paperback) | ISBN 9781534148376 (pdf) | ISBN 9781534151239 (hosted ebook)
Subjects: LCSH: Marine animals–Juvenile literature.
Classification: LCC QL122.2 .D48 2019 | DDC 591.77–dc23
LC record available at https://lccn.loc.gov/2019006019

Printed in the United States of America
Corporate Graphics

CHERRY BLOSSOM PRESS